Honeybees Work Together

Working as a

I0812910

Reggie Harper

COMPUTER SCIENCE For the REAL World™

Rosen Classroom™

Jobs are done quickly when you work as a team. Just ask the honeybee. Honeybees are masters of teamwork!

Honeybees live together in a group called a colony. The colony lives in a hive.

Each honeybee has a special job. They must do their job well for the good of their colony.

Each colony has one queen bee. The queen is the biggest bee. The queen's job is to lay eggs.

Have you ever seen a honeybee?
It was probably a worker bee.
Worker bees are busy all day.

Worker bees fly around looking for food. They collect a yellow dust called pollen from flowers.

Worker bees bring home pollen and nectar. Nectar is a sweet drink found in flowers.

Some worker bees build the hive. The hive is home to the queen, workers, and other bees called drones.

Worker bees also keep the hive clean and safe. They take care of the baby bees.

Honeybees know the power of teamwork. The queen bee and worker bees work together to keep their colony going.

Words to Know

hive

nectar

pollen

queen bee